Hunger

Hunger

poems by Don Stinson

Acknowledgments

Some of these poems appeared, in earlier versions, in the following literary magazines: *Mobius, Riverrun,* and *Phoenix.*

Copyright © 2020 Don Stinson
All Rights Reserved

Cover Art: *up the stairs and to the right*
by Steven Schroeder

Book Design: Rowan Kehn

Turning Plow Press
Ringwood, Oklahoma

ISBN: 978-1-7355762-0-6

As always, for Pam, Caleb, Ethan, and Emily.

For Paul Bowers—poet, publisher, inspiration, and friend.

Dedicated to the memory of all those whom I've lost but who live, at least in my heart and in some of these verses.

Black Dog/White Light

The Black Dog 2
The Black Dog, Loud as Hell 3
The Black Dog Rolls Over 4
The Black Dog Wants a Belly Rub 5
That Morning 6
Upon Reading Dean Young's Comments
    on Emily Dickinson 7
Memo 8
Little Book Rock Room 9
One Magical Day in Tulsa 10
Late Night Last Chance Party 12
"Those are Just Words, Man" 13

Hunger

Hunger 16
Fable 17
Blue is an Illusion 18
Names of Birds 19
Ghosts, Take 1 20
Ghosts, Take 2 21
A Scrap of Paper: 2059 22
A Simple Question on a Simple Night 23
12:01 24
Memory Upon Waking 25
Cosmology, with Merlot 26
The Greatest Country in the World 27
Where the Land Meets the Sea 28
Observational 29
The Bare, Dead Branch by the Side of
    the Road 30
Heterogeneous 31
What Do I Have to Say for Myself? 32

Decades

Poem for Pam 34
Sonnet: 23/07/19 35
Black Shoelaces 36
2x5x3 37
5x3x2 38
Midmorning Scene at Osage Cove 39
Death in the Inland Empire 40
Homegrown Tomatoes 41
Upon Learning of a Friend's Imminent
    Death 42
Victim 43
The Church Janitor 45
The Broken Bandits 46
Oh, You Must Remember *That* Morning 48
A Woman's Book of Days 49
Maybe Just Forgetful 51
Driving to Pryor, Oklahoma, on a
    100-degree Day 52
Decades 53

Ins and Outs

Existential #1 58
Meditation After Breakfast 59
Omega Point 60
666 61
The Lake Where No One Goes 62
Mary M 63
And I Can't Feel At Home in This World
    Anymore 65
Rimbaud in ICU, 1989 66
One Person, One Horizon 67
The Worm Dharma 68
Trinity 69
Confession of a Modern Man 70
For a Seeker 71
Upon a Good Friday 72

I.

Black Dog / White Light

The Black Dog

Sometimes it comes in the door
like a feather on the shoulder
of a shadow.   Other times you turn
and there it stands, or lies, or rolls
over and plays you know what.
Sometimes it's a chihuahua, ridiculous,
too stupid even for self-loathing.
Other time's it's a Dane so great
Hamlet pales, and if you try
to walk it you end up dragged
through the dirt, a bone ready for burial.
Most of the time it's a Bassett Hound,
jowls and ears dragging the ground,
and it casts no shadow, for your shadow
covers it completely, until only its eyes
remain, locking on yours until the dog
enters you like dark steam, and you feel
nothing, nothing at all.

The Black Dog, Loud as Hell

The black dog howls all day,
a hymn of hopelessness breaking
over your brainpan, muted only
by your numb emptiness and vodka.
No bone satisfies. It arches its back
and points its blunt snout
toward the heaven you don't believe in
and wails an aria of alienation,
isolation, blank stares into nowhere.
Finally it falls over on its side,
ribs rising in time with pained pants
sliding toward fitful sleep
filled with black and white dreams
of empty rooms in silent houses,
white faces incapable of recognition,
of cognition, hands swiftly moving to grip
the whip that wakes the beast.
Is it howling, or is that you?

The Black Dog Rolls Over

Occasionally the rolling takes hours,
its hide moving infinitesimally under
your anxious eyes, and you wonder
which way you'll be facing, which way
it, when this process completes, and
the cool of the wood floor flinches
your skin like pool water early in
the morning before the sun rises,
and the rolling begins again.

Other times he rolls so quickly
he disappears for a moment only
to flash back into sight right before you,
eyes fixed on a spot within and yet beyond
you, jaw slack, horrible tongue hanging
like a soul from Charon's bark, and suddenly
he is in you and you in him and your tongue
lolls and you feel the floor beneath you
as you seek the lowest level your life affords.

The Black Dog Wants a Belly Rub

His thick fur folds hold dream worlds.
In this one, pursuing packs,
Chorused howls, rent flesh,
Bones broken under the eye
Of a stoic moon.

Thus is the dream made meat
For the still-living,
For the going on with it,
For the ripples of feeling
Under the master's hand.

That Morning

So that morning you
stepped out of your life

onto clouds sclera white,
far above green blades

hung between trees
rooted in the troposphere

starlings backstroked the air
cat flashed back in tail first

Mandy pulled her tongue
From between your lips

Folded herself under the sheets
Went back to the terrible ex

While you tripped and fell up
Blood soaking into your knees

You grew younger and dumber
Believed in Santa again

As your parents revived
Wise zombies now

But as they clutched together
You felt yourself fade

Into the black hole of
Your father's glassy pupil

Upon Reading Dean Young's Comments on Emily Dickinson

She hurts my head, too,
tongue pressed
on a pained tooth,
knife blade edging
toward the brain
exposed when
the top of your head lifts
off, and you find questions
you never thought to ask,
knowledge you never sought,
solitary in your room,
secure in the walls
of your skull.

Memo

Flowers have eyes, too.
And stones have feelings.
And water has stories to tell
If your pores will listen.

In the densest city
You may stand solitary,
While alone in a field
You're claustrophobic.

All of which is just to say
You're just as screwed up
As all the rest of us.
Did you think you weren't?

Believe me, we all concur.
We've had several meetings.
They were about you.
And you weren't invited.

Little Book Rock Room

I need to book a room
In Little Rock

Or is it

I need to rock a room
In Little Book

Or perhaps

I need room for a book
In Little Rock

On the other hand, it could be

I need a little room
For a book and a rock

Meanwhile, back at the ranch

I need a little book
But with room for a rock

My therapist always says

A little rock needs me
Like a room needs a book

So I have only one final question:

Will you read me like a book
Here alone in this our room
Oh lover my little rock?

One Magical Day in Tulsa

Waiting one day for the light to change,
They might instead decide it never will.
She might open the Lexus' shiny door
And sashay away from Utica Square
Past the I-Hop, Wendy's, and the hospital
Down 21st street, past the park to Peoria,
Where she'd make a left toward Brookside.

Meanwhile, back at the frozen light,
He might reach across her empty seat
And pull to closed that dangling door,
Floor the pedal and race across
The after-all-vehicleless intersection,
Rubber screeching and peeling
Over the summermelt asphalt.

She'd have now walked 20 blocks
To sit in the Brookside Bar
At five o'clock on a Tuesday afternoon
And throw back shots of tequila
While telling anyone who'd listen
Lies about her life as a local actress
Who was an extra in *The Outsiders.*

He'd head north at a high rate of speed,
Take 244 east past the tiny airport,
Merge onto I-44, crowded with cars
Cruising to the Hard Rock Casino
The Cherokees run in Catoosa.
Soon he'd set the cruise on 78,
Follow the signs toward St. Louis.

She'd let some random handsome dude
Take her home and share her bed.
"Well, *that's* done," she'd think,
And she'd never drink tequila again.
She'd get a job teaching kindergarten,
And she'd join the Catholic Church,
And she'd live *someone*'s life, now hers.

He'd barely glance at the famous arch,
Take I-70 through Illinois, Indiana,
Stopping only for coffee and Red Bull,
Popping his last few ADD pills,
Leaving the car in lower Manhattan
Near the exit from the Holland Tunnel,
And walking north on Greenwich Street.

You might say this wouldn't happen,
That people just don't act in this way.
And you'd be right, of course. In fact,
They went home and watched TV,
Got up the next day and went to work.
Wait! There's one other possibility—
Perhaps they're still sitting at the light.

Late Night Last Chance Party

"Where's your blue monkey?"
Yes, that was what she said.
So I wasn't sure if she meant
some kind of exotic drink,
perhaps something with rum,
something that comes on
so sweet, so delicious, so demure,

but often leaves you lying
in a movie-set downpour
in someone else's underwear.
Or maybe, maybe she meant
she wanted to see some part of me
she'd already cutely named,
but I'm quite happily married

and not one part of me's blue,
except sometimes my eyes,
but only in hazy, lazy dreams
that seldom involve monkeys
and from which I awake
to face the strangest questions,
rubbing my eyes with answers.

"Those are Just Words, Man"

Grout is one of those words,
isn't it? Like *kumquat*
or *laissez faire*, one that rolls
not only off your tongue
but out of your mind, where
you're on a surfboard
inspired by Bob Marley
in an ocean
full of motion
with not a shark in sight
and Mother Mary's been praying
for you since the day you were born.

Go ride that wave, the one
swelling and rising like
the inflections of certain syllables,
like *always*, like *simile*,
like *a child's smile*,
like *You really mean it
this time, don't you, and Lover,
oh Lover, so do I.*

II.
Hunger

Hunger

Who knows the flavors of the world
Knows a fleeting tingle of happiness,
The tart taste of sex on the tongue,
The deeper, richer bouquet of love,
Childhood redolent of chocolate and dirt,
The hopeful, fruitful texture of maturity,
The unsweetened applesauce of age,
Heavily spiced to tease the jaded palate.

To taste the world in its variety,
Its buffet of opportunities--better to gorge
Than to pick at the ample offerings.
You can always purge later, go on a diet
And limit yourself, like Byron, to water and bread,
The unfortunate asceticism of the highly bored.

Go on, eat, eat! For the day is coming
When you won't be able to chew a napkin,
When grapes explode into sand in your mouth,
When you cut your meat into tiny well-done pieces
And suck them slowly, with eyes closed,
Remembering the tearing and gnawing
At all the gaudy banquets of your youth.

Fable

Once within a withered time
There somewhat lived a tired man
Who counted his little losses
By piling up the lonely leaves
Clumped around the roots
Of some very rude old trees
Still growing despite all odds
Deep in the deep green heart
Of an odd and ancient wood.
When his losses grew too deep
The wild west wind rushed in
And scattered them to itself
Leaving only roots and silence.

Blue is an Illusion

You reminded me that the sky's not blue,
it's just the way we perceive it. Next
you'll be telling me the grass isn't green,

your eyes aren't brown, my heart's
not shaped like a Valentine's candy,
the President's not a liar, fish bones

aren't a hazard, our children aren't
growing away from us, my eyes aren't
clouding, my hair isn't thinning,

our lives aren't spinning like the hands
on a cartoon clock. But you're right, I know.
Blue is an illusion, like colors, like

advertising, like politics, like other kinds
of love than the one we have, the kind
where we tell each other the truth

and then go look at how blue
the sky can be in Oklahoma
on a certain kind of summer day.

Names of Birds

I do not know
the names of birds
as I should,
as my ancestors
no doubt did
trudging under them
as they trekked
Carolina to Tennessee
on to Arkansas,
shadows of wings
flitting over their heads.

Oh, I know
the garish he-cardinal,
the bully bluebird,
robin with spring's worm
bright in its beak,
quarrelsome grackles
and starlings hording in
fragile branches of sycamores.

But these five flyers
bouncing from powerline
to fence to still-leafless maple—
fighting or flirting, I can't say—
their sudden dance
on a sunny, dismal day
seems otherworldly,
spirits from some old story
told around a campfire
circled by humble wagons
of my ancestors,
who knew the names of birds.

Ghosts, Take 1

I don't believe in ghosts
(other than the many in my head),
though oftentimes my eyes' corners
shimmer in some mystery
when a woman's voice speaks,
when my thinning hair trembles,
when a distant wind murmurs
and my breath, my steps, stop.
Then, I turn around to see
what it is that I cannot see.

Ghosts, Take 2

Do ghosts believe in me?
Imagine them wandering
lost in fading mists of mortality
only to catch a glimpse
of a middle-aged man
staring suddenly at them,
terrible in his need to see.
How frightened they must be,
shimmering, shivering in the cold
where memories of living
and loving die.

A Scrap of Paper: 2059

The last bear lives in my basement.
I feed him drugged squirrels,
Sunday potluck leftovers,
A very occasional honey pot.

He misses the woods, I know,
But they're not safe anymore.
The priests with their bulldozers
Clear space, clear space, clear space.

I think he may be depressed.
He watches TV all day,
Channel-surfing with one shiny claw.
He especially likes the Food Network.

The last bear lives in my basement.
He misses the woods, I know.
I think he may be depressed.
I'd better recheck the lock tonight.

A Simple Question on a Simple Night

Mountains of rain on the horizon
And sky blue day overhead—

The wind brings us its secrets
On the dark arms of the night.

Have you ever heard the voice
Speaking deep within your belly,

Your belly which vibrates to a song?

12:01

Ceramic teapots, chickens, pigs--
knick-knacks on the shelf—
glitter in the midnight glow
from the refrigerator light:
spouts, beaks, snouted bacon
chilling on the China cabinet
containing no cups or plates
Wineglass in your wan hand,
you ease the door closed,
watch that bright wedge
leap across the kitchen wall
one subtle, waltzing step
ahead of sweeping darkness.

Memory Upon Waking

Gracefully they move
through the rooms of the sky
stepping off the clouds
soaring diving without wings
in the corners of the wind
skimming over where I stand
watching, feet heavy as sin,
grounded in the wild-eyed
moment of this dream

Cosmology, with Merlot

Almost eleven-thirty
And this day has passed
Like this wine from this glass.

The stars proliferate,
Though some no doubt die
Millions of years before this moment.

We all leave something
Behind, some shape in air,
Some last blazing before blackness.

All that ultimately endures
Lies in mysterious spaces between,
Pauses between this breath and that.

The Greatest Country in the World

This legendary land lies, of course, quite far away,
Farther than the distance between *now* and *then,*
But when we finally enter its enchanted gates,
We'll learn that the CEO knows the temp's name,
And that the taxis pass right by the bigots
To pick up the trannies and the young black men
On their way to teach peace to the generals' sons
Who by six have memorized the *Tao Te Ching,*
All the works of Whitman and Langston Hughes,
And the Cherokee songs of short love and tall corn.
The flying cars run on dandelions and desire,
And no one knows what "cancer" even *means.*
Everyone gets to be the president for a day
But no one ever needs be a judge. All guns
Fire thick bread, fresh fruit, and sweet wine,
And never run out of their fine ammunition.
The children gleefully flock to their schools,
Gleaming gold on top of the highest hills,
Which of course overlook the cemeteries,
Which are spotless, revered, and joyous,
Filled as they are with music and dance
And the memories of such brief, bright lives.
Best of all, not a single citizen has ever said,
"This is the greatest country in the world."

Where the Land Meets the Sea

Waves came faster, foaming white wishes
through my desert imagination

flying like herons over cattle
grazing deeply in the greenest field

breaking into random molecules
misting our pale Midwestern shoulders

yet we are mesas, cacti, and sun
our memories run like grains of sand

through some stranger's dark and trembling hand

Observational

And who knows the hours
for what they really are
like those who have died?

They watch from afar
as we scamper through,
trailing latte foam and chaos,
certain everything depends
upon what we've still to do.

They shake their dead heads,
sighing without breaths,
watching their clocks
which never move, lamenting
the haste in our dying.

The Bare, Dead Branch by the Side of the Road

(for Emily Stinson)

Emily, you and I have always agreed
that trees are more beautiful, or at least
more interesting, in winter, or at least

when unleaved. Then their branches
become metaphorical in a way
leaves can never be, become

snakes, arms, pleas for mercy, for help,
for signs, for love. Leaves can only fall,
but branches can stretch, reach, hold,

support, extend, ripple in the wind.
And, oh yes, they can snap, break, fall.
And, my daughter, like us in these days,

perhaps all days,
with rage and determination
they can burn.

Heterogeneous

The microscope and the telescope
ultimately peer at each other,
lenses locked on the mystery
seeded in our cells and the stars.
Electrons and galaxies whirl
around hearts thick and dense
with dark illusions of stasis.
A nucleus splits, a sun supernovas,
and somehow we still go on,
eyes clamped tight to the tubes
tying us always to the questions
our instruments strive to answer,
face-to-face on the edge of forever.

What Do I Have to Say for Myself?

Any compulsions, wisdom,
expulsions of rage at the raggedness
of our dire, wired lives?

Memories of hazy afternoons
of beer and sex near
the meandering river? Recollections

of shadowed faces splattered
with sunspots through the hanging leaves,
faces now dead as the friends

who wore them, washed away in the current
toward an unknown ocean
where unlike life motion never ceases?

Formulas, mnemonic devices,
Top 40 hits I hated branded on my brain
like peace, love, and other daydreams.

III.

Decades

Poem for Pam

That hair across the pillow dark
as night as soul as deepest memory
we share and those eyes brown as bark
as earth as the skin of the autumn
and all around us the embrace
of our shared lives and the children
and dogs and that time in Chamonix
when we first found that market
and bought that chicken
the best thing we'd ever eaten
and the sky stretched over Mont Blanc
into an immense moment
I still feel after all these years
as I still feel you as close
as our first night together
as close as if we've never been apart
so many more years with you
than without you and thanks be
for every second, every breath,
every glance across a table in a cafe
where everyone notices
two people looking into each other
and seeing all possible worlds.

Sonnet: 23/07/19

If this should be my last day in this world,
And all my moments left merely a blink,
I hope I have the sense to feel, not think—
The warm, the cool, the wind, the sky unfurled.

What matter then the bank accounts, the rude
And restless rumble of the streets, the news
Of tyrant's tweets? With no time left to lose
Also no space for frantic interlude.

The warmth I seek lies in your lovely lips,
The cool upon your shoulders in the breeze,
The day, each day, remembered as it slips

Into a stream receding through the trees.
If this indeed should be my final day,
So hold me lightly, Love, forever, please.

Black Shoelaces

My favorite boots, black and worn as midwinter night,
Sprawl laceless across the floor, half-leaning
Against the small pine chest-of-drawers.

In them I've dared mountains and shopping malls,
Skipped over rocks crossing rivers,
Hustled my children to school

And sauntered them back home, where, earlier
This slow autumn evening,
You patiently stitched the seams back together,

Leather bowing gracefully and folding under your touch,
As I do. The weaving of your love
Holds strong, running through me,

Pulling me tight, so that even though
I may be worn, sprawling across the floor
With my tongue hanging out,

I know, wise seamstress, that you have,
In the mysterious basket of your smile,
That which will bind me together.

2 x 5 x 3

Lonely pool.
Puffy sky.
Bright night.
You. I.
Vodka tonics,
Sudden quiet.

Far away,
Distant hum
Of traffic
You strain
To hear.

Why bother?
Sudden quiet.
Close by,
Bright night,
You. I.

5 x 3 x 2

Storms in the early morning
Sweep across your sleeping face
Turned toward the open window.

The thunder rocks you awake
And you turn toward me,
All lightning, rain, and wind.

Midmorning Scene at Osage Cove

So strange how rocks piled
like tumbled toys take over
woods, focusing awareness
in this anxious man, morbid,
melancholic. Edges, gaps,
graffiti, recesses—
partially hidden in ferns,
standing watch over stumps,
eternal in a way denied
birds, trees, and someone
finding, in this moment,
something they only later
will remember as peace.

Death in the Inland Empire

Black mascara lashing my mother's face,
Her body braced against grief, she wails
And sobs, beats her fists against the wall
Of my workingman father's chest.

Grandmother's coffin glistens
As smoggy California light
Smirks through the plain windows
Of the Redlands Church of Christ,

And I want Mom to stop,
She's scaring me, she whom
I've never seen cry, never seen sad,
Never seen even close to stopping.

I don't realize her life *has* stopped—
Though only in this hard moment—
I'm four and a narcissist
And I don't remember this dead woman

But I know my mother,
Face contorted with pain,
And I suddenly join her keening,
Childhood dropping from my eyes.

Homegrown Tomatoes

(In Memory of William Lafayette "Fadie" Stinson)

Huge as only memories can be
Red as a cartoon fire truck

Or Superman's billowed cape—
I see Fadie's sharp Old Timer

Halving those bright globes
Again and again into slices

Thick as homemade hamburgers
Or Arkansas' August air.

With salt shakers and short forks
We stormed that storied platter,

Left nothing but pink larval pulp
And a few faintly yellow seeds.

No fruit since then has been
So terrible in its beauty,

The beauty of dying summer
Melting on hungry tongues.

Upon Learning of a Friend's Imminent Death

(In memory of Nila Phipps)

The heart clutches at the words
"lemon-sized tumor,"
a tight fist of thick sorrow.

When I saw you last summer,
with your wig and prosthetic breast,
you still wore that Adair County smile
and that wonderful laugh as you said
you sought a man "looking
for a bald woman with one boob."

I remember your country mother
cooking squirrel dumplings
on a cast iron stove, and how
you loved teaching—no,
not teaching, but your *students*.

Nila, may your journey be easy,
light as ripples on the Illinois River
on a September morning
after autumn's first
so-long-awaited rain.

Victim

Have I not written a poem
about you, dead man,
face down in the dirt,
your wrinkled spirit
sifting with your blood
into the rocky Arkansas soil
you struggled to wring a living from?
Have I never given you a voice,
a chance to tell your Gothic tale,
your father with his anvil eyes,
your mother dead in your birthbed?
Have I never loosened your tongue,
gently wet your parched lips
so that you could speak haltingly
of how the sun caught the shrapnel
that prismed in the light
before burying itself in your shoulder
that day you thought
you'd die on Okinawa?

No, I've covered your mouth
for over forty years,
so long my hand grows stiff
with age and the fear of age
and my heart grows stiff
with rage at the memory
of your murderer's smile
as you settled into the dust
your tongue has become.
I've kept you locked away
from the pens and PCs,
filed away behind jingles
and old girlfriends' parents' names
and my nineteenth phone number,
unable to speak of your fear
when you saw the gun's barrel
lifting toward your shadow
and knew this old enemy
at last for what he was.

Go back to sleep, dead man.
Your services are no longer required.
Each day I feel more like you do.
My stiff hand covers my trembling lips.

The Church Janitor

The dust dances the light descending through
The windows as the boy pushes the broom
Over the worn-out floor between each pew,
Around the silent, empty podium.
His face is round and smooth as the burned light
Bulb he replaces just before he mops,
The summer heat making him sweat, the bright

Drops running down and bouncing off the tops
Of Bibles, hymnals, stray Sunday school texts,
His breath so heavy in the soggy air.
And suddenly he hears a sound. Perplexed,
He listens as he works, can only hear
The children's cries as they play basketball,
The thunk the ball makes on the parking lot,

The whisper of the mop—and that is all.
He shakes his head, and sees he missed a spot.
Washing communion cups he hears a murmur
Like angels praying in the attic loft.
He climbs the creaky ladder, puts an ear
Up to the door, hears nothing but the soft
Rustle of wind, the pumping of his blood,

The snap of neurons in his racing brain
Almost audible in the ancient flood
Of silence rising through the air again.
No one can really say where such thoughts start.
At fifteen, ideas come out of nowhere.
He's locking doors, now ready to depart;
Through the stained glass a billion black eyes stare.

The Broken Bandits
"The Raccoon is of a dark-gray Colour . . . They are rather more unlucky than a Monkey." John Lawson, *A New Voyage to the Carolinas* (1709)

From a distance the blur
on the side of the road
could be a puddle,
a busted tire, an afterthought.
Closer, focus.
Black rings, eyes, tail.
Not a tire busted but
a mother, father, daughter, son—
bandit broken under the wheels.

One, I cluck my tongue.
Two, shake my head.
Three, wonder, stunned.
Four, count the dead.

Diggers, dousers, the one
who rubs, scrubs, scratches,
the one the Japanese call "washing bear."

I once knew a Cherokee woman
who stopped and prayed for roadkill,
dragged them off the asphalt
into the grass, into the trees,
to decompose with dignity.
People thought her crazy,
I thought her saint.
"God's little creatures," she'd say,
"deserve at least a few words."

I'm no saint and seldom pray,
but remember that night
driving with my wife
down Turkey Mountain in Tulsa,
those two raccoons who stopped
in the middle of the road, so
I stopped, waited,
and that night prayed
them safely on their way.

Perhaps those were my few words,
offerings to those more deserving.

Oh, You Must Remember *That* Morning

A sore neck, an empty wallet,
stains of dubious origin—
a good time was had, and yet
emptiness remains, lurking
in the milliseconds between
memory and embarrassment.

With coffee, reality returns,
and the longing for a cigarette
still, after 20 smokeless years.
You stub that dull urge out
on the blunt edge of your love,
this desire that feeds, keeps you.

Mornings have always chafed—
as a child you hid your head
under the covers of your bed
and waited for the daylight
to settle in around you
the way it's still settling.

A Woman's Book of Days

Sunday's supposed to be the day of rest—
instead I'm racing to make it to church,
fighting with kids to get them dressed,
too stressed by the time we finally arrive
to breathe a proper prayer.

Monday's definitely the worst—
shoveling the walk so the girls can catch the bus
because *he's* got a "bad back"
(damaged, no doubt, from too many twelve-ounce curls),
then a long day at that trapdoor to hell we call an office.

Tuesday the car breaks down,
and I spend the money for Molly's braces
to get it fixed, so I can make it to work
to listen to Les blame women and immigrants
for ruining the country he loves.

Wednesday we make love madly
in the space between chores and bed,
and forget for a few minutes the leaky toilet,
the budget crisis, the way the neighbors
look away now when we pull in.

Thursday, I get a letter
from a distant old friend
and discover she's lost her mother,
and, though we haven't spoken in years,
soak the neat handwriting with my tears.

Friday everything goes right,
so right I buy a Powerball ticket
when I stop for gas and wine on the way home.
He makes his spaghetti—his only dish—
and we eat Rocky Road at midnight in bed.

Saturday I realize I'm getting old—
it sneaks up like the snow flakes
that started early this morning,
gray hairs in the brush, the weeks
coiled and shining amidst the bristles.

Maybe Just Forgetful

Every day
I feel my mind
moving farther away
to a place
I don't want
to recognize.
My mother lived there
for many years
in a land of shadows,
echoes, dropped names
and identities.
I reassure myself
it'll be different
for me, with my books,
my three degrees, my
"active life of the mind."
But the dice roll
as they will
across the gaming table,
and I'll see only sevens
showing as long
as I am able to recall
what follows five and six.

Driving to Pryor, Oklahoma, on a 100-degree Day

Steaming cattle lumber
from the pond
toward shifting shade
beneath the cottonwood
where they lie, fly-tortured
monoliths mechanically
chewing their cuds
through the long heat.

Do they miss spring,
wish for fall as I do,
restless and depressed
through endless July?
No birds circle a pale sky,
at least none visible
from a Honda's back seat,
my daughter at the wheel.

Trees and grasses beside
the road shimmer greenly
beneath the sun, reaching
blades and limbs upward
through the heavy air.
You can be better, they
whisper, eyes turning
suddenly toward mine.

Decades

At 1

Who knows? A shadowy photo exists—
I a shirtless toddler staring into a lens
Under a merciless August Arkansas sun,
Mother gussied up in her Sunday best
Holding me against her shoulder,
So Father must have snapped the shot
Then waited weeks for a meager payday
To purchase the picture's development
At some Fort Smith photo shop
Long gone, like Mother and Father.

At 11

Beginning my last year in California
(Though unaware of that at the time)—
All I really remember is the bomb blast
From across the street, the hippie boy
Running across the yard with bloody stumps
Where his radical hands had once been,
That image and my father's coughing
Predicting that everything would change,
That we would flee that desert chaos
In a futile attempt to find some kinder home.

At 21

I'm almost certain this was the year
I fell into the madness of young love (again),
Also the year that a friend, a Vietnam vet,
Attacked me with a broken whiskey bottle
And I ran until the memory of that moment
Was left far enough behind that I exhaled
And found myself outside under high stars
Blinking in the soft Oklahoma night,
Winking at me as if to say, "Yeah, you,
You are somehow a survivor."

At 31

Writing reviews of community theater,
Fretting over my pregnant wife, frail life
Growing inside her as mine morphed into
Some unforeseen semblance of manhood,
Responsibility, teaching students to write
And reading all night, scribbling verse
Under the influence of so much fluid love
That even today my hands still shake
When I remember those moments,
Those first movements under her belly.

At 41

I'd finally made it to Europe, where Pam and I
Lay in a narrow bed in a narrow room, but
By God we could see the Eiffel Tower
If we leaned together in just a certain way.
By then we'd leaned together for over a decade,
And found three children formed from our bones,
Our blood, our desire. We were moving then,
As we did so often in those ancient days,
Stepping on Legos in the darkness of night,
Praising our lives through our sudden curses.

At 51

Those children? They thankfully grew up,
And we found ourselves in the middle of life
Still in a town we'd planned to someday leave
But had instead come to some days love,
One of so many tricks up life's harlequin sleeve.
Hello to new jobs, goodbye to old friends,
More ends but even more beginnings amidst
The swirls and eddies of each passing day,
Light and darkness fighting within me still
And heavy footsteps always at my back.

At 61

Looking out my office window at winter clouds,
Missing our children, all gone though not too far,
Not yet, the madness of young love long adjusted
Into the bonds of so much caring, such sharing
As I would gladly wish upon you all, as I curl
My legs under my desk and write these lines
Staring at pictures of poets, places, loved ones—
So much forgotten, yet so much recalled,
Formulas of a long-gone youth, song lyrics,
Shudder of Mother's shoulder before the flash.

IV.

Ins and Outs

Existential #1

If it is indeed true
That the first bomb
Dropped on Germany
during World War II
killed the only elephant
in the Berlin Zoo,
then I am again humbled
before an absurd God.
How mysterious His ways?
Give me a fucking break.
Forget His ways, his means,
His inscrutable theology.
Our lives are as random
As blips on a radar,
Dark spots on an MRI,
Radio static on the dish
Searching for alien life—
As pointless as the rain drop
Sliding down the elephant's trunk
The moment before.

Meditation After Breakfast

Sometimes the world seems
a wonderful little idea
in the mind of a happy fool,
a bit of a lark, a folly,
a fanciful experiment in lust
and need and near-collisions.
On those days it's best
to take the sun as it's given
and find a quiet place
inside or outside yourself
to hide away the moments,
your own private heaven,
the only one you'll ever own.

Omega Point

All our roads ultimately converge
Into a tunnel whose end cannot be seen.

No one has ever reached that end,
As the tunnel extends with every breath,

With every death, into a future
Where we may not know each other

As human, or even remember
Exactly what that used to mean.

Our linked minds may briefly ponder
The splendor of our gleaming bodies,

Washed in starshine and time,
Moving slowly forward together

To whatever's beyond the end.

666

Radio's gone silent.
The end wasn't violent.
I saw the white moon rise
Over the blasted fields.
Faint light bled through the skies.
Love's the last hope that yields.

The Lake Where No One Goes

If the Holy Spirit exists, persists
Within this busy world of tangled woes,
That Ghost dwells soundlessly within the mists
Rising at dawn from the shores where no one goes.
The sensitive mind scans the horizon
For signs that all is not metal and meat—
A reason compels the elision
Of tragicomedy's bitter and sweet.
But that lake is hidden so far away,
And life, both short and long, so distracting,
The mind ignores the lake for one more day,
Mists where spirit slowly keeps retracting.
Minds trudge one, down the well-worn, rutted road,
Holding that nothing that's such a heavy load.

Mary M

She watched Him, wishing
She knew what He was—
A man of course, yet nothing
Like the many men she'd had.

Once she had been insane,
They said, tormented, cursed.
He had touched her;
Her mind had cleared.

Joanna and Susanna
Just laughed at her
When she confessed her love,
Though He had touched them, too.

"He doesn't like girls," they giggled.
"He's got twelve boyfriends."
She covered her ears.
Mary wept.

When they killed Him,
She couldn't watch.
But she followed the soldiers
To the tomb and waited.

When the earth shook, and the angel
Told her He had risen,
She expected that now
Any miracle could happen—

That he might even marry,
Settle down in Galilee,
With a fallen woman.
After all, He didn't judge.

But he rose farther
Than she'd ever thought.
And she was left
To disappear into history

Alone, remembering
Little things—the touch on her hair
Of His hard carpenter's hands,
The magical taste of fish and bread

Salty in her mouth,
The way He looked at her
As He waved, just before
He vanished into a cloud.

And I Can't Feel At Home in This World Anymore

The swivel-necked owl
high in the barren elm
just might be God,
yellow eyes sharp
as memories of Eden,
watchful gaze pivoting
over all the earth,
hanging in a tree,
our ready savior,
ready—when he sees
a streak in the field—
to drop like hymns,
crush faithless bones.

Rimbaud in ICU, 1989

Another night of nasty pain and sweat pissing from you into your sad pillow.
You'd notify local authorities of your situation if only there were any.
Too late for all that drama now, too late for dread as the moon's below
Your shrinking horizon. Your remaining options now few, once many.

You vaguely recall the coming here, the clownish pratfalls face-first into now:
A woman or man in tears, clear vodka over ice, children, children and blood;
A nurse with yellow syringe and yearning smile, an actor with smirking bow,
Something always about loss, a whole world flushed in a sudden flood.

The idiot sun stumbles in from the east wing, but this stage is empty
Save for you with your ridiculous jungle of hanging bags, tubes and wires,
Hovering huge faces filled with perfect teeth you paid for. It can't be.
Another night has always, always been. Trust no one. These people are liars.

You push the blessed, fascist button and for a moment it all fades
And you pretend as you have so often pretended, it truly seems forever,
To believe in the profoundest nothing, no shining paradise, no Hades.
A pretender no more, you know you'll never again disbelieve. Never.

One Person, One Horizon

Trees' fingers spider a dusky flatline
somewhere out there is California
and an ocean
eyes can't make it that far
fences demand attention

Wallenda squirrels tightrope the evening
into spectacles of derring-do and
nothing-short-of miracles
miracles like those words
you said yesterday

which have aged gracelessly
into the echoes of this evening
where bored servers contemplate suicide
in the shadow of the question to all answers
which has haunted us since we learned

to examine everything
and found ourselves so alone
we could hardly believe we existed
outside of the mind of that god
thriving on our meager offerings

The Worm Dharma

Three days of warm, thin rain
Bring worms from nowhere
Into the small, marshy yard.
Some seem as big as snakes,
Wriggling between the drops
Drifting from a dull low sky.
I step between their dark curves
Like a cautious Buddhist monk,
Moving toward a distant sun
Crawling behind the clouds
Clotted thickly as the desires
Crowding the path to wisdom.

Trinity

The first day of spring has sprung
in this familiar manner,
a ramble of green grass, buds,
cloudlessness and restlessness,
as if motion alone may
redeem March the 20th.
I sweep floors, missing my wife.

The two dogs seem sleepier,
sluggish except at mealtime
as if winter-exhausted.
So many tasks await me
I don't know where to begin.
I've ignored all my email,
polished my best coffee cup.

My inner flame burning low,
my inner voice strangely mute,
I watch the maple's robins
and squirrels through the window
as the sun floats behind clouds.
Today, the first day of spring,
can my soul now learn to sing?

Confession of a Modern Man

Bless me Mother
for I have sinned
against Thee
and Father Sky

I've neglected
to properly notice
when last-gasp winter
gives way to Spring

I've quite forgotten
the birdsong language
the melodies of breeze
branching through air

Forgive my inattention
my wandering mind
Teach me Thy wisdom
the child's laugh on the wind.

For a Seeker

And if the light that shines so brightly
turns out to be merely afterglow,
and the truth that has sustained you
reveals itself as one more dead end,
don't despair, my pilgrim friend. You
will go back to the beginning again,
and relearn there how to walk,
the way to lace words into prayer,
off-key notes into joyous hymns,
stumbling acts into graceful works,
and another light will illuminate
the Truth already deep within you.

Upon a Good Friday

Where once we needed to name
The nomenclature of nature,
Delineating fir from pine from spruce,
Where at a glance the dance
Of prairie grass denoted
Breeze from gust from simple wind,
Where we searched the clouds for clues,
The cumulus, cirrus, ominous walls,
Telling us all we needed to love or fear,
Where even then we envied the silent,
Those few who knew the secret codes
That made them quiet together,
Like pines blown by wind under clouds.

www.ingramcontent.com/pod-product-compliance
Lightning Source LLC
Chambersburg PA
CBHW021130080526
44587CB00012B/1225